GREEN BOND MARKET SURVEY FOR THAILAND

INSIGHTS ON THE PERSPECTIVES OF INSTITUTIONAL INVESTORS AND UNDERWRITERS

JUNE 2022

ASIAN DEVELOPMENT BANK

ADB

CONTENTS

Table, Figures, and Boxes   iv

Acknowledgments   vi

Abbreviations   vii

Summary and Key Findings   viii

INTRODUCTION   1
Background and Objective   1

Methodologies   1

OVERVIEW OF THAILAND'S SUSTAINABLE BOND MARKET   2

RECENT INITIATIVES ON SUSTAINABLE FINANCE   5

SURVEY RESULTS   11
Institutional Investors   11

Advisors and Underwriters   18

WHAT ADB CAN DO TO HELP   26
As a Knowledge Partner   26

As an Investor   26

FINAL WORD BY RESPONDENTS   28

NEXT STEPS   29

TABLE, FIGURES, AND BOXES

TABLE

Thai Green Bond Market Investor and Underwriter Portfolios by Sector   ix

FIGURES

1   Sustainable Bonds Outstanding in the Thai Market by Issuer Type   2

2   Sustainable Bonds Outstanding as Shares of Sustainable Finance Market   3

3   Issuance Currency of Sustainable Bonds Outstanding   3

4   Local Currency Sustainable Bonds Outstanding as a Share of the Local Currency Bond Market   4

5   Sustainable Information Platform Webpage   6

6   Interest in Investing in Green Bonds   11

7   Optimal Investment Size   12

8   Share of Investor Portfolios with an Investment in Green Sectors   12

9   Key Motivations for Investing in Green Bonds   13

10   Main Obstacles Preventing Investors from Investing in Green Bonds   13

11   Key Considerations for Investing in Green Bonds   14

12   Policy Mechanisms That Would Increase Green Bond Investments   14

13   Level of Local Investor Interest by Issuer Type   15

14   Sectors with Most Potential for Green Bond Investments   15

15   Policy Options for Green Bond Market Development   16

16   Capacity Building—Who Should be Trained?   17

17   Investor Interest in Regional Investment   17

18   Preferred Underlying Currencies   17

19   Investor Perception of the Potential of Sustainability-Linked Bonds   18

20   Investor Interest in Sustainability-Linked Bonds   18

21   Structure of Local Advisors and Underwriters Responding to the Survey   19

22   Current Market Shares of Leading Underwriters in Thailand   19

23   Interest in Issuing Green Bonds   19

24   Optimal Issuance Size   20

25   Sectors That Are Most Promising Sectors for Green Bonds Issuance   20

26   Key Motivations for Issuing Green Bonds   21

27   Main Obstacles Preventing Issuers from Investing Green Bonds   21

28   Key Drivers for Green Bonds Issuance   22

29   Preferred Investors in Green Bonds   24

30   Preferred Policy Options for Green Bond Market Development among Advisors and Underwriters   24

31   Capacity Building—Who Should be Trained?   25

32   Potential of Sustainability-Linked Bonds to Turn Brown Companies Green   25

BOXES

1   The Asian Development Bank's Journey into Green Bonds and Blue Loans in Thailand   23

2   The Asian Development Bank's Technical Assistance to Support Thai Issuers and Underwriters   27

ACKNOWLEDGMENTS

The lead authors—Kosintr Puongsophol, financial sector specialist; Oth Marulou Gagni, senior operations assistant; and Alita Lestor, consultant; all of the Economic Research and Regional Cooperation Department (ERCD) of the Asian Development Bank—would like to particularly thank Satoru Yamadera, advisor, ERCD; Richard Supangan, senior economics officer, ERCD; Noel Peters, principal investment specialist (climate finance), Private Sector Operations Department (PSOD); Daniel Wiedmer, principal investment specialist, PSOD; Krittayamon Paocharoen, senior investment officer, PSOD; and Rob Fowler, consultant for their support and contributions. Editing by Kevin Donahue. Design and layout by Prince Nicdao.

The lead authors would like to thank the Global Green Growth Institute team, comprising Srinath Komarina, Hien Tran, Thinh Tran, Minh Tran, and Ha Nguyen for their inputs and suggestions.

Finally, we would like to express our heartfelt gratitude to the Thai regulatory authorities and industry associations, as well as to all respondents, for their assistance with and participation in the survey. The local regulatory authorities include the Bank of Thailand; Office of the Insurance Commission; Securities and Exchange Commission, Thailand; and Stock Exchange of Thailand. Industry associations include the Association of Securities Companies, Association of Investment Management Companies, Thai Bankers Association, and Thai Bond Market Association.

ABBREVIATIONS

ABMI	ASEAN+3 Asian Bond Markets Initiative
ADB	Asian Development Bank
ASEAN	Association of Southeast Asian Nations
ASEAN+3	ASEAN plus the People's Republic of China, Japan, and the Republic of Korea
BOT	Bank of Thailand
ESG	environmental, social, and governance
LCY	local currency
OIC	Office of the Insurance Commission
SEC	Securities and Exchange Commission, Thailand
SET	Stock Exchange of Thailand
SDG	Sustainable Development Goal
SLB	sustainability-linked bond
SLL	sustainability-linked loan
TA	technical assistance
ThaiBMA	Thai Bond Market Association
THB	Thailand baht
USD	United States dollar

SUMMARY AND KEY FINDINGS

▶ The survey was conducted in November 2021 via an online platform and received a total of 41 responses from 12 asset management firms, 6 commercial bank treasuries, 12 financial advisors and underwriters, and 11 insurance companies.

▶ While all respondents (investors and underwriters) expressed interest in investing in and underwriting green bonds, some may be more prepared to do so than others. This is an area where development partners such as the Asian Development Bank can potentially assist interested entities with technical assistance and capacity building.

▶ Renewable energy, energy efficiency, and clean transportation are viewed as the most promising sectors for growth in Thailand's green bond market.

▶ While there is a strong preference for small green projects (less than USD50 million) from investors' point of view, underwriters and advisors are hoping for much bigger deals (more than USD100 million).

▶ Both investors and underwriters consider the lack of a green project pipeline as a major impediment to the green bond market's development in Thailand.

▶ While nearly 100% of investors believed that a mandated external review is critical, less than 60% of underwriters agreed.

▶ The majority of respondents believe that sustainability-linked bonds will be one of the key drivers for brown companies to become green.

▶ Development banks can play a variety of roles in catalyzing growth of the green bond market.

The green bond market in Thailand has potential to expand further. The majority of institutional investors and underwriters are interested in green bonds and in taking the necessary actions to either increase their green portfolio or underwrite more green bonds.

Capacity building is crucial. The majority of respondents agreed that it is critical to continue building capacity among relevant stakeholders, particularly finance officers of listed companies, investors, and underwriters. Board members of state-owned enterprises should also be trained to a lesser extent, as these enterprises can contribute to market development by issuing sustainable bonds. Additionally, this is consistent with the governments' bio-circular and green policies.

Renewable energy, energy efficiency, and clean transportation are the sectors with the highest growth potential. Respondents agreed on the importance and potential of renewable energy, energy efficiency, and clean transportation. Indeed, these sectors already account for the majority of investors' portfolios in the Thai green bond market (**Table**).

Table: Thai Green Bond Market Investor and Underwriter Portfolios by Sector (%)

Investors			Underwriters		
Renewable Energy	Clean Transportation	Energy Efficiency	Renewable Energy	Clean Transportation	Energy Efficiency
25	23	16	32	27	24

Source: Survey results.

A clear investment mandate and the expansion of eligible issuers are important. More than 90% of survey respondents believed that to increase investment in green bonds, they must incorporate environmental, social, and governance principles and the Sustainable Development Goals into their investment strategies. Meanwhile, both underwriters and investors shared the same view that it is critical to expand the pipeline of green projects and attract new issuers, particularly corporate issuers from the renewable energy and clean transportation sectors, to green bond markets. Governments and regulators can catalyze market development by incentivizing investors, improving disclosure requirements, and developing standardized green definitions.

Demand from investors is extremely important. Underwriters believed that increased demand from investors is crucial to encourage more issuance of green bonds. In fact, preferential buying by public pension funds and central banks would demonstrate leading by example. They also believe that tax incentives and/or subsidies for issuers is equally important.

Unlike underwriters, investors have a strong preference for smaller investment sizes. Almost 50% of investors are looking for an investment size of less than USD10 million per transaction, and 40% are interested to invest up to USD50 million. On the other hand, almost 70% of underwriters are looking for issuance sizes of more than USD100 million.

A green image is important. Nearly 100% of investors and underwriters agreed that investing in and issuing green bonds can help an organization improve its green image. From investors' point of view, investing in green bonds allows them to better diversify their portfolios, while issuers hope that issuing green bonds will result in lower funding costs, albeit not immediately, but potentially in the long run.

External review is important to create more demand. While nearly 100% of investors believe that an external review report is necessary for making informed investment decisions, less than 60% of underwriters agree. This may be because engaging an external reviewer incurs additional costs for issuers, particularly pure-play issuers focused exclusively on green projects. Based on survey responses, it is clear that an external review can allow issuers to diversify their investor base.

Development partners can play an important role in promoting green finance. All respondents agreed that development partners such as the Asian Development Bank (ADB) can play a variety of roles in assisting Thailand's green finance market development. Along with serving as a knowledge partner, ADB can provide technical assistance to assist local companies in issuing green bonds and identifying eligible green projects and expenditures. Additionally, ADB can invest in green bonds and/or make green loans to domestic entities.

INTRODUCTION

Background and Objective

The Asian Development Bank (ADB) is collaborating closely with the Association of Southeast Asian Nations (ASEAN), the People's Republic of China, Japan, and the Republic of Korea—collectively known as ASEAN+3—to promote the development of local currency (LCY) bond markets and regional bond market integration through the Asian Bond Markets Initiative (ABMI). ABMI was established in 2002 to bolster the resilience of ASEAN+3 financial systems by developing LCY bond markets as an alternative source to foreign-currency-denominated, short-term bank loans for long-term investment financing.

ADB, as secretariat for the ABMI, is implementing a regional technical assistance (TA) program to promote sustainable LCY bond market development. This TA was developed and is being implemented with guidance from ASEAN+3 finance ministers and central bank governors, in accordance with the ABMI Medium-Term Road Map for 2019–2022.

This survey report, conducted in collaboration with the Global Green Growth Institute, aims to assess institutional investors' interest in green bonds issued in Thailand, as well as the perspectives of local arrangers and underwriters on their clients' interest in green bond issuance. The survey aimed to identify market drivers, impediments, and development priorities for Thailand's sustainable finance market to assist development partners in identifying potential areas of support to accelerate the development of Thailand's sustainable finance market.

Methodologies

In November 2021, ADB and the Global Green Growth Institute conducted the survey via an online platform and received a total of 41 responses from 12 asset management firms, 6 commercial bank treasuries, 12 financial advisors and underwriters, and 11 insurance companies.

OVERVIEW OF THAILAND'S SUSTAINABLE BOND MARKET

Thailand's sustainable bond market has grown rapidly in recent years, particularly since the Securities and Exchange Commission, Thailand (SEC) introduced regulations allowing the issuance and offer for sale of green bonds in late 2018 and social and sustainability bonds in the middle of 2019. These were the first steps taken toward developing Thailand's sustainable bond market.

Sustainable debt instruments, according to the SEC, were not new types of instruments, but rather debt instruments with a specific use of proceeds for projects that contribute to positive environmental and social outcomes. As a result, in addition to the requirement to comply with international standards and practices governing sustainable bonds, existing regulations applicable to the issuance of debt securities were used to supervise the issuer of such sustainable debt securities. The SEC issued regulations related to the issuance and offer for sale of sustainability-linked bonds (SLBs) in May 2021, which were later revised in September 2021, to further develop the capital market's key role in contributing to resolving social and environmental issues and promoting the sustainable development of businesses in various industries through alternative sustainable finance products. These SLB regulations—like those for green, social, and sustainability bonds—are based on internationally recognized standards and include references to traditional debt securities regulations.

The total outstanding amount of green, social, and sustainability bonds in Thailand was USD5.7 billion at the end of December 2021, with private sector issuances leading the way (**Figure 1**).

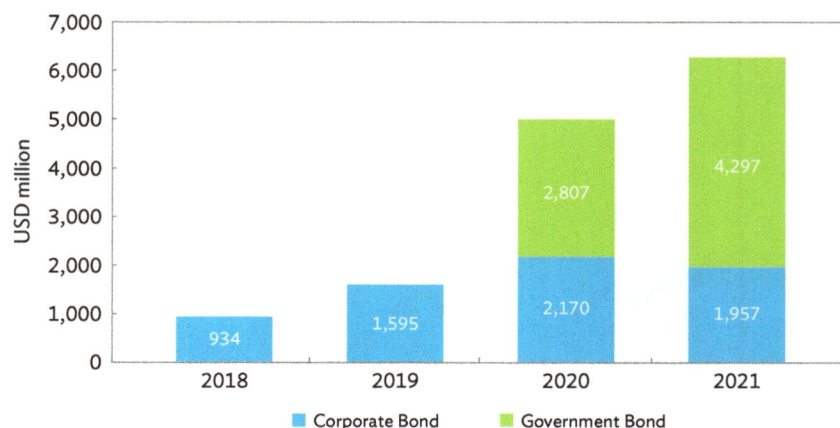

Figure 1: Sustainable Bonds Outstanding in the Thai Market by Issuer Type

USD = United States dollar.
Note: All data as of 15 March 2022. Data were obtained using Bloomberg LP's SRCH function. The SRCH criteria included green bonds, social bonds, sustainability bonds, sustainability-linked bonds, and transition bonds.
Sources: *AsianBondsOnline* and Bloomberg LP.

Green bonds are the most common type of sustainable bond in the Thai market, followed by sustainability bonds (**Figure 2**). Except for one state-owned financial institution, the Bank for Agriculture and Agricultural Cooperatives, which issued a nongovernment-guaranteed green bond in August 2020, the majority of green bond issuers are corporations. The Government of Thailand's sustainability bond, on the other hand, dominates the sustainability bond market. In August 2020, the Public Debt Management Office, with ADB assistance, issued the country's first sustainability bond in two tranches totaling THB30 billion (approximately USD964 million). The bond was three times oversubscribed, and the proceeds will be used to fund green infrastructure and social impact projects. The bond carried a 1.585% interest rate, which was lower than the current market yield on a 15-year benchmark bond at the time. The bond has been reopened on a regular basis by the Public Debt Management Office, and its outstanding value was THB197,000 billion as of 18 March 2022.

The social bond market began to emerge following the issuance of a social bond by the National Housing Authority in 2020. While corporations can contribute to social development, there is a lack of awareness among many corporate issuers. In November 2021, Thaifoods Group became the first nonfinancial corporate issuer in ASEAN to issue a social bond. The bond proceeds were lent to subsidiaries for the purpose of financing and refinancing projects and assets related to job creation and economic advancement in local communities.[1]

In terms of currency, the majority of the sustainable bonds have been issued in Thai baht (**Figure 3**). This demonstrates the importance of the LCY bond market in providing liquidity to domestic corporations and the government when seeking to raise funds, particularly as the country seeks to achieve the Sustainable Development Goals (SDGs) in the aftermath of the COVID-19 pandemic.

Figure 2: Sustainable Bonds Outstanding as Shares of Sustainable Finance Market

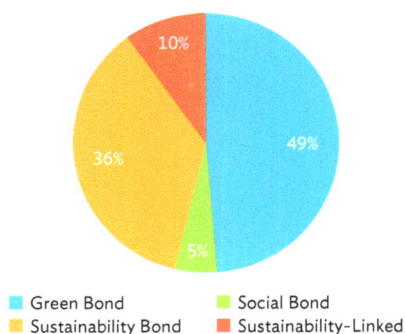

- Green Bond — 49%
- Sustainability Bond — 36%
- Social Bond — 5%
- Sustainability-Linked — 10%

Note: All data as of 15 March 2022. Data were obtained using Bloomberg LP's SRCH function. The SRCH criteria included green bonds, social bonds, sustainability bonds, sustainability-linked bonds, and transition bonds.
Sources: *AsianBondsOnline* and Bloomberg LP.

Figure 3: Issuance Currency of Sustainable Bonds Outstanding

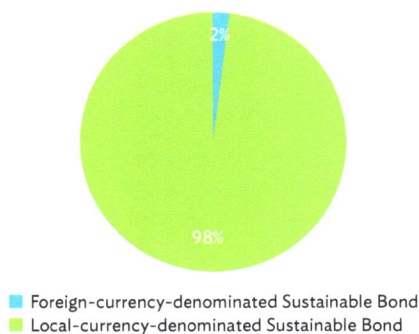

- Foreign-currency-denominated Sustainable Bond — 2%
- Local-currency-denominated Sustainable Bond — 98%

Note: All data as of 15 March 2022. Data were obtained using Bloomberg LP's SRCH function. The SRCH criteria included green bonds, social bonds, sustainability bonds, sustainability-linked bonds, and transition bonds.
Sources: *AsianBondsOnline* and Bloomberg LP.

[1]   ADB. 2021. First Social Bond Issued by Nonfinancial Corporate Issuer Under ASEAN Social Bond Standards. News release. 17 November.

Despite its rapid expansion, the sustainable bond market remains small in comparison to the country's overall LCY bond market (**Figure 4**). Sustainable bonds accounted for only 1.8% of total LCY bonds outstanding as of December 2021. However, this number is rapidly growing, demonstrating the numerous opportunities to promote more issuance of LCY sustainable bonds in the country.

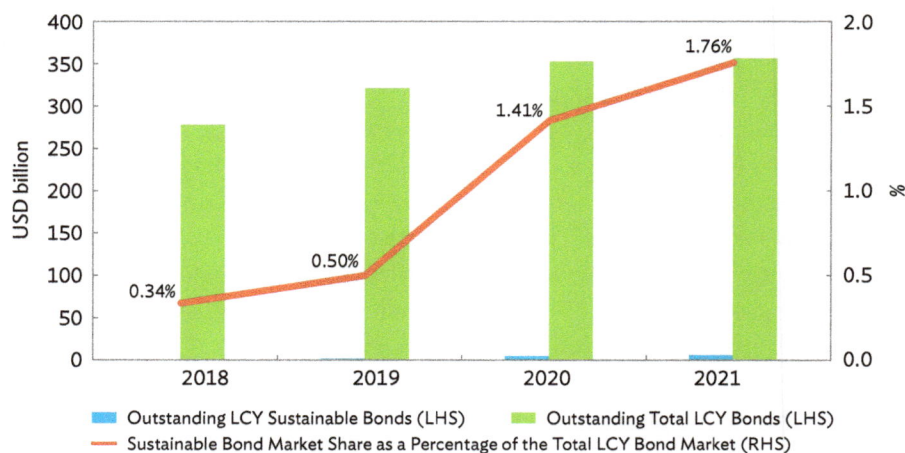

Figure 4: Local Currency Sustainable Bonds Outstanding as a Share of the Local Currency Bond Market

LCY = local currency, LHS = left-hand side, RHS = right-hand side.

Notes: Data were obtained using Bloomberg LP's SRCH function. The SRCH criteria included the following details green bonds, social bonds, sustainability bonds, sustainability-linked bonds, and transition bonds. Bonds issued by central banks are excluded.

Sources: *AsianBondsOnline* and Bloomberg LP.

RECENT INITIATIVES ON SUSTAINABLE FINANCE

One of the top priorities of Thai policymakers and financial market regulators is to promote sustainable finance. The Fiscal Policy Office, Bank of Thailand, Office of Insurance Commission, Stock Exchange of Thailand (SET), and SEC formed a Working Group on Sustainable Finance to collaborate on the sustainable finance agenda and support the Thai economy in achieving the SDGs and meeting carbon emissions reduction targets.[2] On 18 August 2021, the Working Group on Sustainable Finance jointly published *Sustainable Finance Initiatives for Thailand* to set the direction and framework for driving sustainable finance across the financial sector. The document recommends five key strategic initiatives:

(1) Developing a Practical Taxonomy
(2) Improving the Data Environment
(3) Implementing Effective Incentives
(4) Creating Demand-Led Products and Services
(5) Building Human Capital

This section includes a summary of key initiatives being undertaken by relevant regulators.

Sustainable finance is prioritized in the *SEC Strategic Plan, 2021–2023* and one of several initiatives that contribute to Thailand's sustainable capital market ecosystem. For example, in January 2021, the SEC declared support for and became an official supporter of the Task Force on Climate-Related Financial Disclosures.[3] In so doing, the SEC aims to raise awareness and encourage the business sector to incorporate climate-related risks into their strategic planning and risk management and follow international standard disclosure guidelines. This will strengthen the Thai capital market's ability to contribute to sustainable development in line with Thailand's *National 20-Year Strategy* and the SDGs.

Most recent, the SEC published the *SEC Strategic Plan, 2022–2024*, which aims to achieve three main objectives: (i) enhancing competitiveness, (ii) ensuring inclusiveness, and (iii) strengthening trust and confidence in the Thai capital market. Among five key results outlined in the strategic plan, the SEC seeks to strengthen the capital market's capacity for sustainability through the following measures:[4]

---

[2] See Bank of Thailand. Sustainable_Finance_Initiatives_for_Thailand.pdf (bot.or.th).

[3] See SEC. 2021. SEC Becomes a Supporter of the Task Force on Climate-Related Financial Disclosures. *SEC News*. 15 January.

[4] See SEC. English (United States) News Detail.

(1) Enhancing Environmental, Social, and Governance practices to be on par with international standards
  (a) promoting carbon neutrality in accordance with Thailand's commitment announced at the Conference of the Parties' World Leaders Summit in Glasgow in November 2021,
  (b) conducting due diligence with regard to human rights, and
  (c) promoting implementation of the United Nations SDGs among listed companies and relevant capital market stakeholders.

(2) Promoting integration of Environmental, Social, and Governance in business operations
  (a) issuing environmental risk management guidelines

for fund management companies and analysts,
  (b) issuing guidelines to encourage the incorporation of sustainability considerations into the operations of fund management businesses companies, and
  (c) organizing capacity-building programs for regulated entities.

The SEC also launched the Investment Governance Code, which contains guidance reflecting internationally accepted standards for responsible investment. Moreover, the SEC and the Thai Bond Market Association (ThaiBMA) collaborated to design and launch the Sustainable Information Platform to serve as an information center for green, social, and sustainability bonds and SLBs. The platform will enhance the visibility of sustainability-themed products (**Figure 5**).[5]

Figure 5: Sustainable Information Platform Webpage

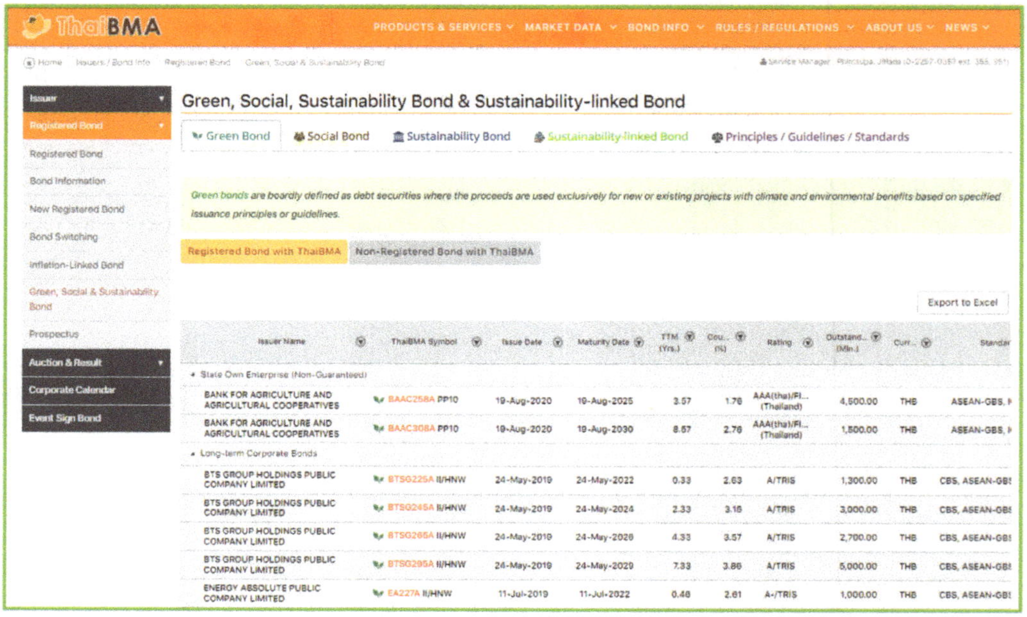

Source: Thai Bond Market Association.

---

[5]   See ThaiBMA. Green, Social, and Sustainability Bonds.

The Sustainable Information Platform is a one-stop source of information on all sustainable bonds issued by Thai entities, both domestically and internationally. It contains information about a bond's key characteristics and links to the issuer's frameworks and external reviewer reports, as well as internationally accepted standards and guidelines on the issuance and offering of green, social, sustainability bonds, and SLBs.

In 2019, the SEC waived approval and filing fees for green bonds, social bonds, and sustainability bonds issued between May 2019 and May 2022. This incentive was also expanded to include SLBs upon the implementation of the Notification of the Capital Market Supervisory Board (Tor Jor. 31/2564) Re: Application and Approval for Offer for Sale of Newly Issued Sustainability-Linked Bonds in May 2021. On 3 March 2022, the SEC board approved the extension of this incentive through 31 May 2025 and removed restrictions on the use of proceeds from green bonds, social bonds, and sustainability bonds. Previously, the proceeds must be used in Thailand and neighboring countries. This restriction has been removed from the new incentive in favor of promoting business operations that help address global climate change. Similarly, the ThaiBMA announced that the application fee for green, social, and sustainability bonds issued would be waived, in accordance with SEC regulations, and the annual fee would be reduced by THB10,000 per year, effective from 26 March 2019 to 28 June 2020. This incentive was extended through June 2022 and expanded to include SLBs.

On 4 April 2022, the SEC issued regulations for the disclosure standards of the Sustainable and Responsible Investing Fund to widen access for retail investors. The regulation allows investors to compare between mutual funds with similar sustainability mandates and, as a result, be able to make informed investment decisions. For instance, fund managers are required to disclose the fund's sustainability objectives, sustainability targets, investment strategies, and underlying security selection, among other things. The new regulation came into effect on 1 April 2022.[6]

Furthermore, all listed companies on the SET will need to disclose their sustainability information integrated with their business reporting in a format known as "One Report," which covers issues such as carbon emissions and human rights. In 2015, the SET created the Thailand Sustainability Investment list for investors seeking an alternative investment in high-performing environmental, social, and governance (ESG) stocks while also supporting sustainable Thai businesses. The SET defines sustainable businesses as those that balance risk management, supply chain management, and innovation with ESG responsibilities.[7] To complement the Thailand Sustainability Investment list, the SET launched the Thailand Sustainability Investment Index in 2018, which consists of high-performing stocks from an ESG standpoint, in order to attract investors interested in the responsible investment trend. Furthermore, Thai listed companies of all sizes will be encouraged to adopt the ESG concept, with the goal of increasing their visibility in global sustainability indices, raising global investor awareness. Through its Sustainable Capital Market Development Initiative, the SET also organizes various training programs and provides sustainable business development tools for listed companies to integrate SDGs in their operations.

---

[6]   See https://www.sec.or.th/TH/Pages/News_Detail.aspx?SECID=9376.

[7]   See SET.SET Index Series.

The Thai Bankers Association introduced the *Sustainable Banking Guidelines for Responsible Lending* to advance Thailand's sustainable banking practices.[8] These are voluntary sustainable lending guidelines that establish minimum standards for sustainable lending practices while also taking members' sustainability strategies and business models into account. Given the banking sector's dominance in Thailand, this development is extremely welcome, as financial institutions' active involvement in sustainable finance is a critical component of the ecosystem for financing the country's sustainable development. This also enables financial institutions to more effectively manage and analyze their portfolios' exposure to financial risks associated with climate change.

The Bank of Thailand's (BOT) *Strategic Plan, 2020–2022: Central Bank in a Transformative World* identifies sustainability as one of seven strategic challenges that must be addressed effectively over a 3-year period.[9] As part of its reserves management, the BOT continues to diversify investment risk in its portfolio and regularly expands the number of countries and asset classes included in the investment universe, including assets that contribute to positive environmental and social outcomes.

During the United Nations Climate Change Conference in November 2021, the BOT expressed its support for the Network of Central Banks and Supervisors for Greening the Financial System's Glasgow Declaration: Committed to Action, which outlines the network's commitment to strengthening the financial system's resilience to climate-related and environmental risks and encourages the scaling-up of financing flows necessary to support the transition to a sustainable economy.

In February 2022, the BOT conducted market consultations, with the findings summarized in *Repositioning Thailand's Financial Sector for a Sustainable Digital Economy*.[10] The objective of this consultation was to lay out the important directions and policies for repositioning the Thai financial sector in a new landscape and to seek feedback to ensure that the new landscape appropriately serves the needs of all stakeholders. The consultation paper outlines the following key objectives:

(1) The financial sector leverages technological advancements to drive innovation and provide inclusive financial services and consumer protection, in a level playing field and competitive environment.

(2) The financial sector facilitates the transition of businesses and households to a digital economy and helps them effectively manage environmental risks.

(3) The financial sector is resilient to significant and new risk factors and able to contain systemic risks in rapidly changing environments without transmitting them to the system or consumers at large.

One of the key focuses of the new landscape is managing the transition toward sustainability. It aims to steer the financial sector to systematically incorporate environmental considerations into their operations and to offer financial products that facilitate businesses' adaptation and transition away from

---

8   See TBA Guidelines of Sustainable Banking.

9   The BOT's Strategic Plan, 2020–2022 is available from the BOT website at https://www.bot.or.th/English/AboutBOT/ RolesAndHistory/DocLib_StrategicPlan/BOT-StrategicPlan2020to2022-eng.pdf.

10   See Bank of Thailand. Consultation-Paper-en.pdf (bot.or.th).

environmentally unsustainable activities without disrupting the economy. These aspirations are in line with the nation's goal of achieving carbon neutrality by 2050 and net-zero emissions by 2065. Key policies include the following:

(1) Develop a Thai taxonomy to promote the development of a national green taxonomy.
(2) Set disclosure standards so that financial institutions can demonstrate their commitments and actions on environmental sustainability in a manner that is clear and consistent with international standards, such as those recommended by the Task Force on Climate-Related Financial Disclosures.
(3) Promote financial products to support the transition by actively encouraging the introduction of new financial services and products that help businesses adapt and transition away from activities that are environmentally unsustainable.
(4) Create the right incentive structures with mechanisms or measures to help alleviate the burden or cost of adjustments for financial institutions and businesses to facilitate timely transitions.
(5) Build capacity of financial sector personnel to increase competencies and skills in the financial sector.

More details will be disclosed in the directional paper, *Managing Transition towards Greater Environmental Sustainability*, which is scheduled to be released in the second quarter of 2022.

As a key member of the Working Group on Sustainable Financing, the Office of the Insurance Commission (OIC) is promoting good ESG practices among insurance companies and throughout the industry. Although the issue of sustainability is relatively new to the global insurance industry, the OIC recognizes the critical nature of the effects of climate change and social issues on the sector. When preparing its strategic plan for the insurance sector's development, the OIC took these concerns into account. The OIC's sustainability initiatives are concentrated in four critical areas:[11]

(1) Incorporate sustainability into the OIC's strategic plan, which includes the adoption of measures regulating insurance companies on sustainability-related issues.
(2) Facilitate the development of sustainable insurance products, particularly those that aid in managing economic risk, agricultural output, and providing equal access to life and nonlife insurance products for all members of society.
(3) Allow insurance companies to invest in environmentally friendly financial products such as investment-grade green bonds or stocks of companies with sound ESG practices that are listed on both domestic and international stock exchanges, including responsible investment funds.
(4) Provide capacity building to raise awareness and educate the insurance industry about the importance and significance of environmental and social impacts. Insurance literacy is a critical component of the *Third Insurance Development Plan, 2016–2020*.

---

[11] See คปภ. จัด ESG กำกับธุรกิจประกันให้ยั่งยืน (thansettakij.com).

Additionally, the OIC's *Fourth Insurance Development Plan, 2021–2025* emphasizes the importance of the insurance sector in contributing to the sustainable development of economic and social systems.[12] To advance ESG principles, priorities include promoting the development of insurance products that benefit the environment, such as tree insurance to encourage tree planting. Insurance companies may also consider lowering premiums for green businesses and electric vehicles. In terms of incentives, the OIC encourages insurance companies to operate in accordance with ESG principles through tax measures and will reward insurance companies that do so.

---

[12]   See OIC. The Insurance Development Plan Vol. 4.

SURVEY RESULTS

The survey was conducted in November 2021 among local institutional investors—including fund managers, financial institutions, insurance companies—and local underwriters and advisors. A summary of the survey's findings is given below.

Institutional Investors

The survey began by asking asking respondents about their firms' interest and/or current investment in green financial instruments. The majority of respondents indicated there was interest in green financial instruments and that their respective firms are currently developing an action plan, while others were exploring this field but with limited awareness and resources (**Figure 6**). None of the respondents indicated a lack of interest in green bonds. One asset management company reported having established green bond positions despite not having developed green bond mandates. Further, two insurance companies expressed a strong interest in green bonds and both have established a green investment mandate.

Due to the fact that the majority of respondents are still developing an action plan, green bonds account for less than 5% of their aggregate portfolios. Only one respondent, an asset management firm, indicated that green investments accounted for between 11% and 20% of its total portfolio.

When asked about ticket size, 45% of respondents indicated a preference for investments of less than USD10 million, while

Figure 6: Interest in Investing in Green Bonds

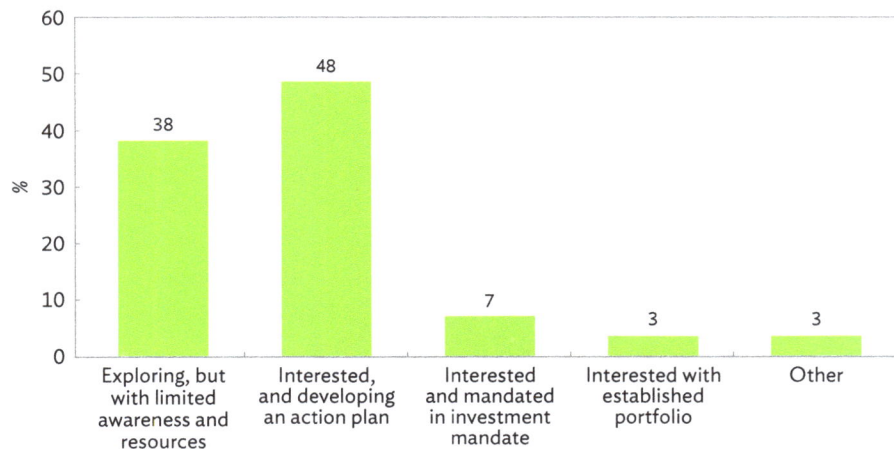

Source: Authors' compilation based on survey results.

38% indicated a willingness to invest up to USD50 million per transaction (**Figure 7**). Only 3% of respondents indicated that they were flexible in terms of ticket size, stating that it is determined by yield.

In terms of sector preference, renewable energy (25%), clean transportation (23%), and energy efficiency (16%) are the top sectors in respondents' investment portfolios (**Figure 8**). Meanwhile, almost 10% of respondents have no exposure to green investments, while only 4% of respondents have invested in green bonds issued to finance green buildings.

When respondents were asked about their primary reasons for investing in green bonds, the majority of investors believe that this would give them an opportunity to integrate an SDG mandate into their institution's investment strategy (**Figure 9**). Almost 100% of respondents also shared that investing in green bonds would improve the green image of their organization. Meanwhile, institutional investors believed that investing in green bonds would help them diversify their portfolios effectively.

To help ADB and local regulators support the development of green bond markets, investors were asked to identify any major obstacles to investing in green bonds. Almost 40% of respondents stated that the primary impediment is a lack of pipeline projects and interested issuers. This clearly indicates that Thailand's current supply of green bonds is insufficient to meet demand; as a result, there is a significant opportunity for issuers to consider green bond issuance as a means of diversifying

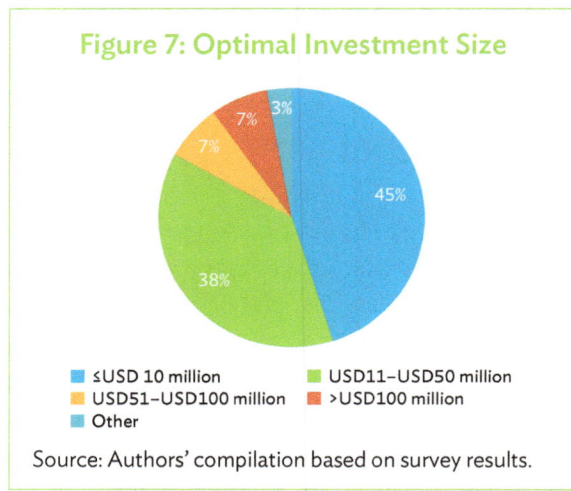

Figure 7: Optimal Investment Size

Legend:
- ≤USD 10 million
- USD11–USD50 million
- USD51–USD100 million
- >USD100 million
- Other

Pie values: 45%, 38%, 7%, 7%, 3%

Source: Authors' compilation based on survey results.

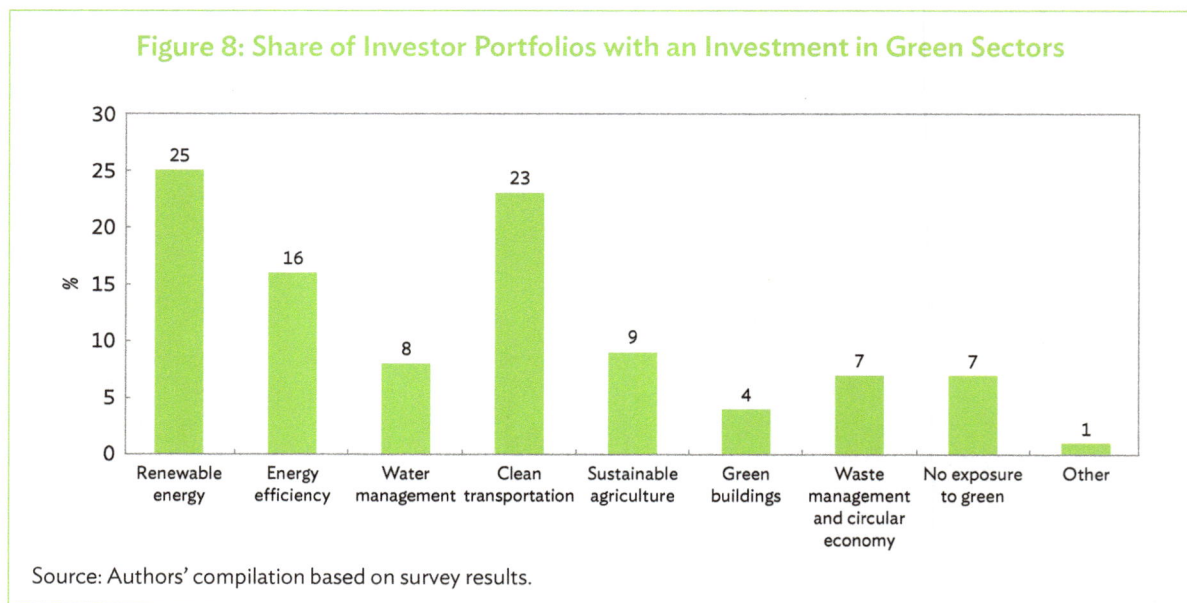

Figure 8: Share of Investor Portfolios with an Investment in Green Sectors

Sector	%
Renewable energy	25
Energy efficiency	16
Water management	8
Clean transportation	23
Sustainable agriculture	9
Green buildings	4
Waste management and circular economy	7
No exposure to green	7
Other	1

Source: Authors' compilation based on survey results.

Figure 9: Key Motivations for Investing in Green Bonds

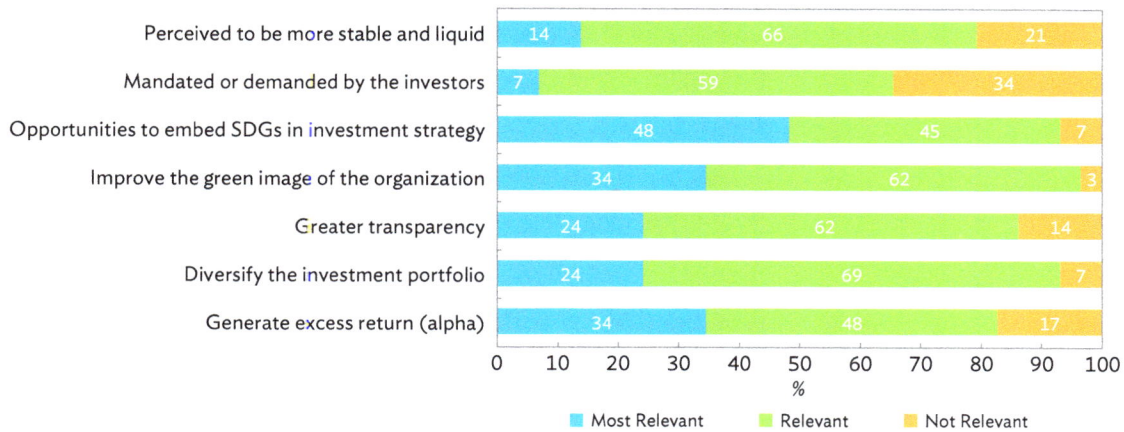

Perceived to be more stable and liquid — Most Relevant: 14, Relevant: 66, Not Relevant: 21
Mandated or demanded by the investors — Most Relevant: 7, Relevant: 59, Not Relevant: 34
Opportunities to embed SDGs in investment strategy — Most Relevant: 48, Relevant: 45, Not Relevant: 7
Improve the green image of the organization — Most Relevant: 34, Relevant: 62, Not Relevant: 3
Greater transparency — Most Relevant: 24, Relevant: 62, Not Relevant: 14
Diversify the investment portfolio — Most Relevant: 24, Relevant: 69, Not Relevant: 7
Generate excess return (alpha) — Most Relevant: 34, Relevant: 48, Not Relevant: 17

■ Most Relevant   ■ Relevant   ■ Not Relevant

SDG = Sustainable Development Goal.
Source: Authors' compilation based on survey results.

their investor base. Based on the information published on ThaiBMA's ESG information portal, only 11 Thai companies have issued green bonds thus far, with aggregate issuance of THB80 billion (approximately USD2.4 billion). Additionally, 25% of respondents indicated that the absence of clear benefits from investing in green bonds was one of the key inhibiting factors, while nearly 20% indicated that the absence of regulatory guidance on green bonds is also an impediment. Around 6% of respondents also suggested that having the right tenor and currency is also relevant (**Figure 10**).

When investing in green bonds, investors continue to prioritize credit ratings (**Figure 11**). This is unsurprising, given that the majority of green bonds are issued by corporate issuers.

Figure 10: Main Obstacles Preventing Investors from Investing in Green Bonds

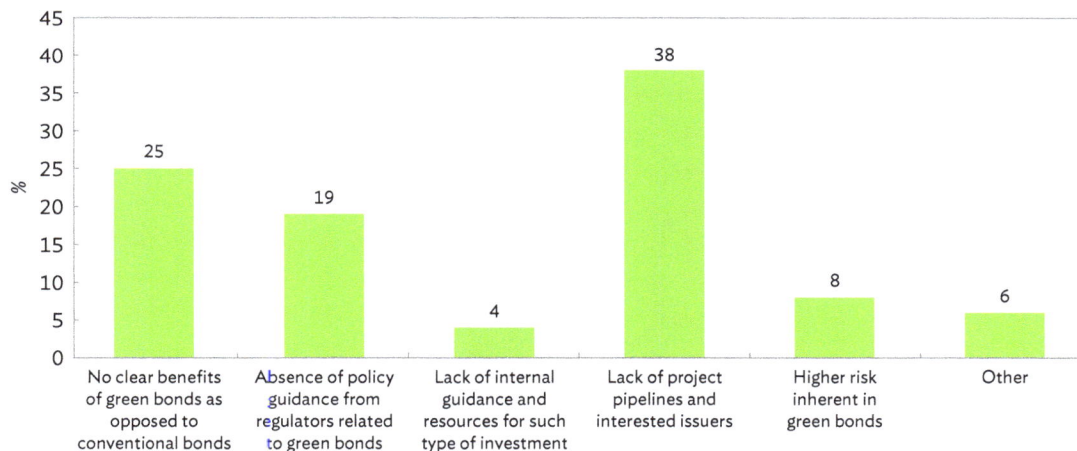

No clear benefits of green bonds as opposed to conventional bonds: 25
Absence of policy guidance from regulators related to green bonds: 19
Lack of internal guidance and resources for such type of investment: 4
Lack of project pipelines and interested issuers: 38
Higher risk inherent in green bonds: 8
Other: 6

Source: Authors' compilation based on survey results.

Figure 11: Key Considerations for Investing in Green Bonds

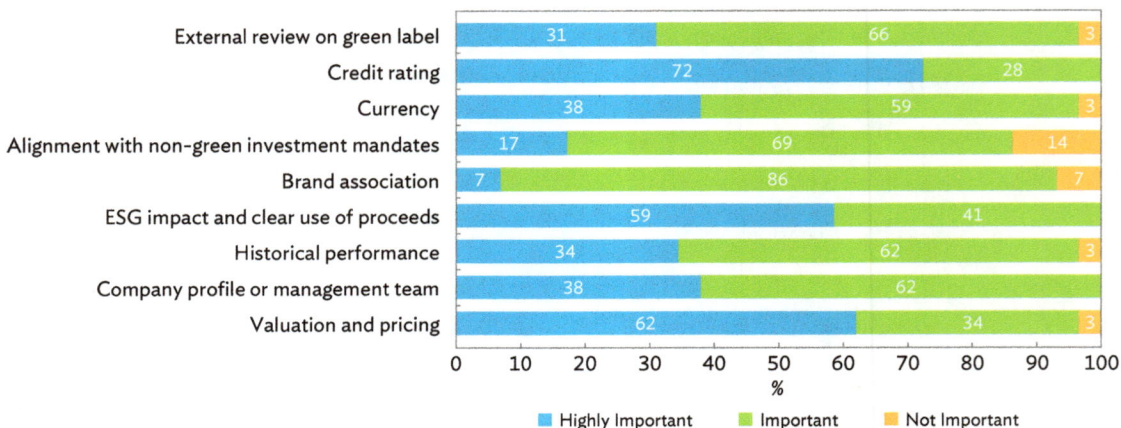

	Highly Important	Important	Not Important
External review on green label	31	66	3
Credit rating	72	28	
Currency	38	59	3
Alignment with non-green investment mandates	17	69	14
Brand association	7	86	7
ESG impact and clear use of proceeds	59	41	
Historical performance	34	62	3
Company profile or management team	38	62	
Valuation and pricing	62	34	3

ESG = environmental, social, and governance.
Source: Authors' compilation based on survey results.

The second most critical factor is the bond's price and coupon, as these directly correlate to the bond's credit rating. The third priority is the ESG impact of the bond and how the issuer intends to use the proceeds to benefit the environment. The majority of investors believe that external review by a third party is critical and would aid them in making investment decisions.

To address these issues, respondents were requested to select up to three options that they felt could encourage the growth of Thailand's green bond market. Nearly 30% of respondents recommended that the government implement tax incentives and/or subsidies to entice investors to hold more green bonds (**Figure 12**). Meanwhile, nearly 20% of responses indicated that increased ESG disclosure by

Figure 12: Policy Mechanisms That Would Increase Green Bond Investments

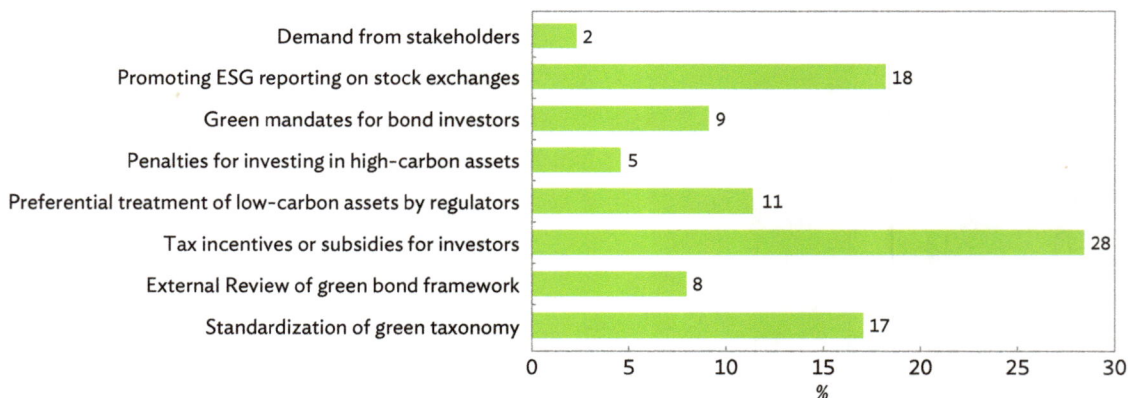

	%
Demand from stakeholders	2
Promoting ESG reporting on stock exchanges	18
Green mandates for bond investors	9
Penalties for investing in high-carbon assets	5
Preferential treatment of low-carbon assets by regulators	11
Tax incentives or subsidies for investors	28
External Review of green bond framework	8
Standardization of green taxonomy	17

ESG = environmental, social, and governance.
Source: Authors' compilation based on survey results.

listed companies, as well as a clear taxonomy defining what constitutes green assets, projects, and expenditures, would significantly assist investors in making green investment decisions.

As previously stated, investors believe that the domestic supply of green bonds issued in Thailand is insufficient to meet their demands. The survey investigated which types of issuers of green bonds respondents are interested in. Local institutional investors indicated that they

are most interested in corporate issuers, such as nonfinancial institutions, followed by the sovereign government and financial institutions (**Figure 13**). In terms of sectors, almost 25% of responses believe that renewable energy and low-carbon transportation offer the greatest investment potential in Thailand (**Figure 14**). This finding is consistent with the sector breakdown of respondents' current portfolios of green assets.

Figure 13: Level of Local Investor Interest by Issuer Type

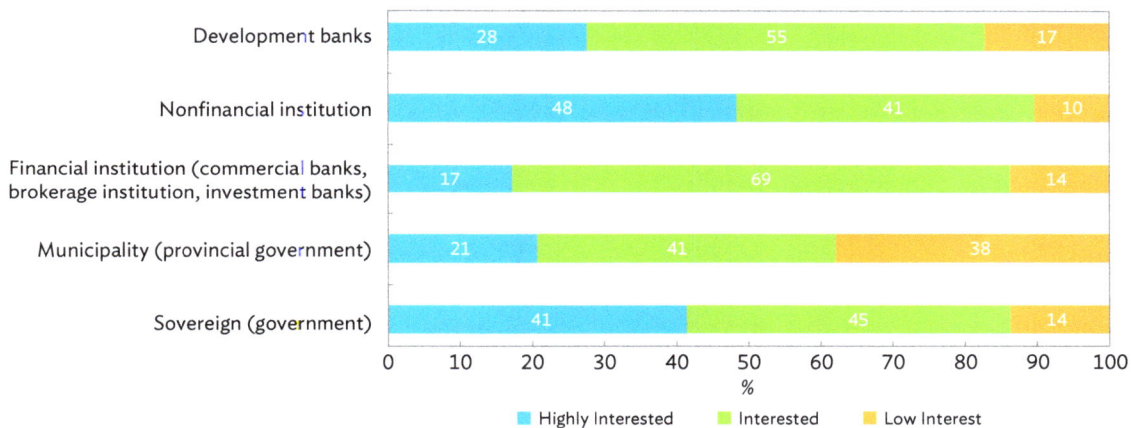

Source: Authors' compilation based on survey results.

Figure 14: Sectors with Most Potential for Green Bond Investments

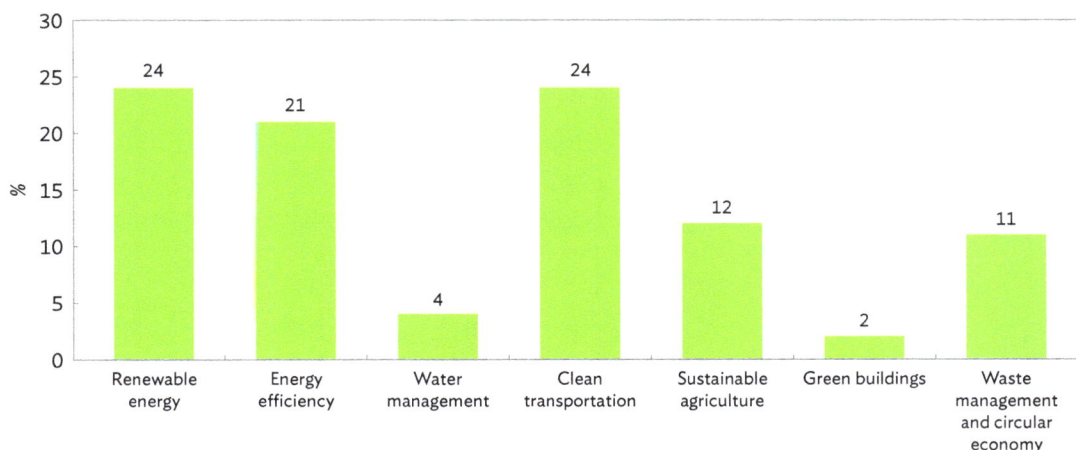

Source: Authors' compilation based on survey results.

On policy options to develop the green bond market, all respondents emphasized the critical importance of government and regulatory policy clarity to increase private financing. Indeed, nearly 70% of respondents believed this to be the most important factor. Among the objectives of this policy guidance are the establishment of clear guidelines for green bond issuance procedures, the enhancement of the reporting framework, and the disclosure of green bonds. The SEC has published several green and other types of sustainable bond issuance guidance, which are accessible on the SEC's website.[13]

Respondents believed that having a clear definition of "green" would provide industry guidance on which green investments are eligible (**Figure 15**). Additionally, this would enable potential issuers to assess and ensure that their existing projects, assets, and expenditures conform to green bond standards and principles. Almost 100% of respondents believed that green bonds should be properly labeled, thus external review should be mandated in regulations. In

doing so, they also believed that subsidies to cover external review fees should be provided to encourage labeling of green bonds. Respondents commended the SEC and ThaiBMA for their efforts in developing a centralized ESG information portal on the ThaiBMA website to provide information on green, social, sustainability, and SLBs in Thailand, with 38% finding it extremely useful and 59% finding it useful. Furthermore, respondents also believed that a subsidy for labeling green bonds or green loans is also important.

Regarding capacity development, respondents unanimously agreed that investors require additional training (**Figure 16**). Additionally, it was felt that chief financial officers of listed companies should be trained to gain a better understanding of green bonds. This would lead to an increase in the supply of green bonds to meet investor demand.

The majority of Thai investors have no intention of investing in the region (**Figure 17**). Singapore, Viet Nam, and Indonesia are the preferred

Figure 15: Policy Options for Green Bond Market Development

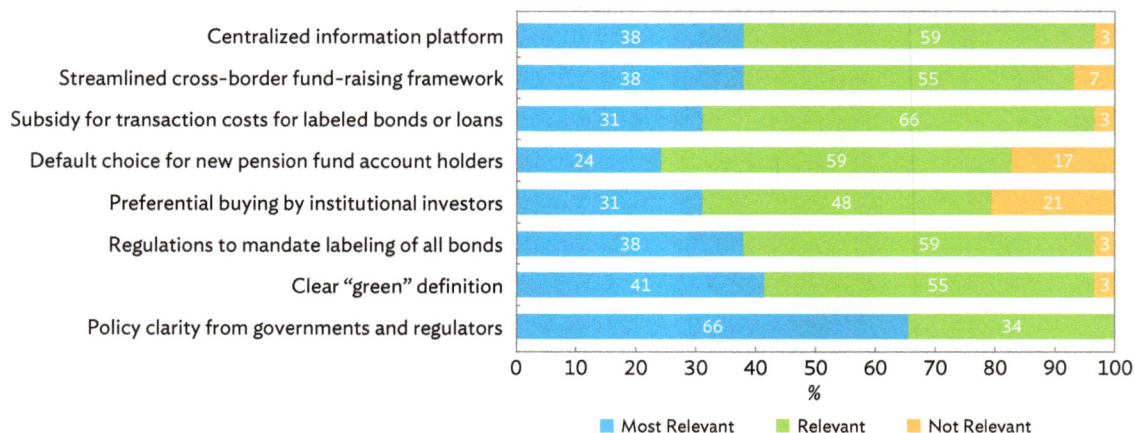

	Most Relevant	Relevant	Not Relevant
Centralized information platform	38	59	3
Streamlined cross-border fund-raising framework	38	55	7
Subsidy for transaction costs for labeled bonds or loans	31	66	3
Default choice for new pension fund account holders	24	59	17
Preferential buying by institutional investors	31	48	21
Regulations to mandate labeling of all bonds	38	59	3
Clear "green" definition	41	55	3
Policy clarity from governments and regulators	66	34	

Source: Authors' compilation based on survey results.

---

[13] See SEC. Thai Resource Center.

Figure 16: Capacity Building—Who Should Be Trained?

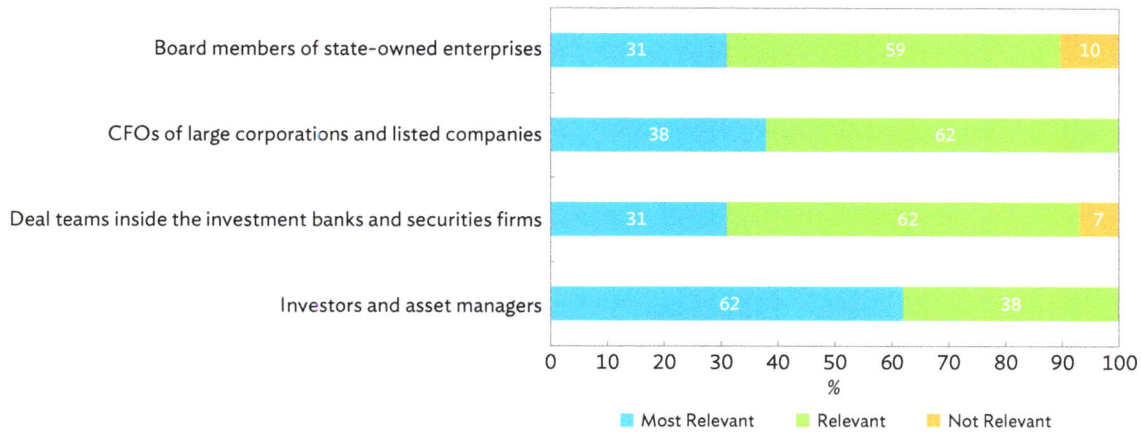

	Most Relevant	Relevant	Not Relevant
Board members of state-owned enterprises	31	59	10
CFOs of large corporations and listed companies	38	62	
Deal teams inside the investment banks and securities firms	31	62	7
Investors and asset managers	62	38	

■ Most Relevant   ■ Relevant   ■ Not Relevant

CFO = chief financial officer.
Source: Authors' compilation based on survey results.

investment destinations for those interested in regional investment. When asked about the underlying currency, over 80% of respondents preferred hard currencies such as the United States dollar, euro, and yen (**Figure 18**).

Per the International Capital Market Association, SLB refers to "any type of bond instrument

for which the financial and/or structural characteristics can vary depending on whether the issuer achieves predefined sustainability [or] ESG objectives. In that sense, issuers are thereby committing explicitly (including in the bond documentation) to future improvements in sustainability outcome(s) within a predefined timeline. SLBs are a forward-looking

Figure 17: Investor Interest in Regional Investment

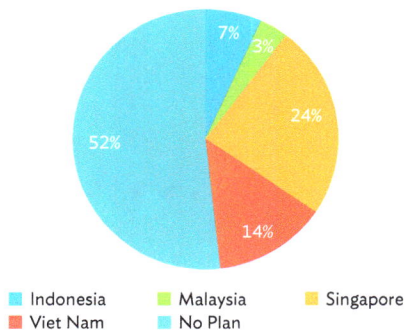

- 52% Indonesia
- 7% Malaysia
- 3% Singapore
- 24% Singapore
- 14% Viet Nam

■ Indonesia   ■ Malaysia   ■ Singapore
■ Viet Nam   ■ No Plan

Source: Authors' compilation based on survey results.

Figure 18: Preferred Underlying Currencies

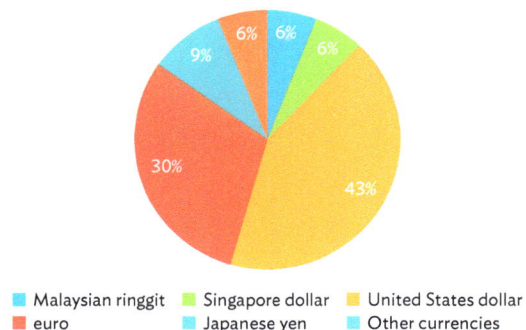

- 6% 6% 6%
- 9%
- 30%
- 43%

■ Malaysian ringgit   ■ Singapore dollar   ■ United States dollar
■ euro   ■ Japanese yen   ■ Other currencies

Source: Authors' compilation based on survey results.

14   See ICMA. 2020. Sustainability-Linked Bond Principles. June.

performance-based instrument."[14] Meanwhile, sustainability-linked loans (SLLs) "are any types of loan instruments and/or contingent facilities (such as bonding lines, guarantee lines, or letters of credit) which incentivize the borrower's achievement of ambitious, predetermined sustainability performance objectives."[15] For both SLBs and SLLs, the issuer or borrower's performance is measured through predefined key performance indicators and assessed against predefined sustainability performance targets.

When asked about new financial instruments such as SLBs and SLLs, more than 97% of respondents believed that SLBs and SLLs could act as a catalyst for brown companies to become green (**Figures 19** and **20**). Around 97% of respondents indicated that they will most certainly invest in SLBs and SLLs. Indeed, nearly 40% of respondents indicated that they have already invested in SLBs or SLLs.

The SEC issued the SLB regulation in May 2021 and revised it again in September 2021.

Advisors and Underwriters

This section examines the interest of potential green bond issuers, most promising economic sectors, and various types of potential issuers based on responses from local advisors and underwriters.

Overview of the Respondents

Out of 12 respondents, the majority of them are commercial banks and their subsidiaries (**Figure 21**). This is aligned with the local market environment in which commercial banks are the primary underwriters of corporate bonds in the Thai market. **Figure 22** presents the market shares of corporate bond underwriters for long-term corporate bond (excluding long-term bill of exchange, promissory notes, and self-issue).

Respondents' clients are generally interested in and are developing plans for green bond issuance. Several clients have already issued green bonds, while others are exploring the

Figure 19: Investor Perception of the Potential of Sustainability-Linked Bonds

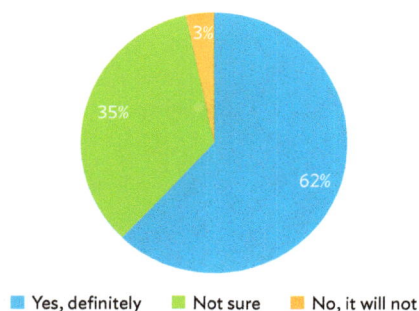

- Yes, definitely — 62%
- Not sure — 35%
- No, it will not — 3%

Source: Authors' compilation based on survey results.

Figure 20: Investor Interest in Sustainability-Linked Bonds

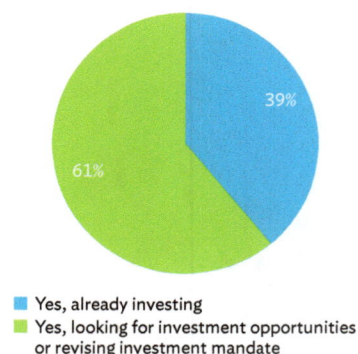

- Yes, already investing — 39%
- Yes, looking for investment opportunities or revising investment mandate — 61%

Source: Authors' compilation based on survey results.

---

15   See LSTA. Sustainability-Linked Loan Principles.

Figure 21: Structure of Local Advisors and Underwriters Responding to the Survey

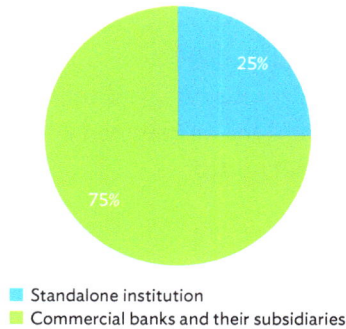

- Standalone institution
- Commercial banks and their subsidiaries

Sources: Survey results and Thai Bond Market Association.

Figure 22: Current Market Shares of Leading Underwriters in Thailand

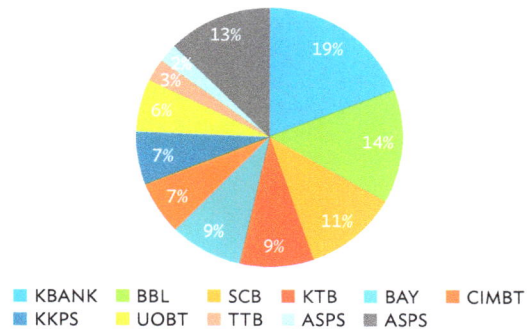

- KBANK ■ BBL ■ SCB ■ KTB ■ BAY ■ CIMBT
- KKPS ■ UOBT ■ TTB ■ ASPS ■ ASPS

ASPS = Asia Plus Securities Company Limited,
BAY = Bank of Ayudhya Public Company Limited,
BBL = Bangkok Bank Public Company Limited,
CIMBT = CIMB Thai Bank Public Company Limited,
KBANK = Kasikornbank Public Company Limited,
KKP = Kiatnakin Phatra Bank Public Company Limited,
KTB = Krung Thai Bank Public Company Limited,
SCB = Siam Commercial Bank Public Company
Limited, TTB = TMBThanachart Bank Public Company
Limited, UOBT = United Overseas Bank (Thai) PLC.
Sources: Survey results and Thai Bond Market Association.

possibility but lack the necessary resources and awareness. This may be an area where development partners such as ADB can assist interested entities with technical assistance and capacity building. It was encouraging to learn that none of the respondents indicated their clients are opposed to green bond issuance (**Figure 23**).

In terms of issuance size, almost 70% of respondents indicated that optimal issuance size for green financial instruments is greater

than USD100 million, while 8% of respondents shared that the optimal deal size should be between USD300 million and USD500 million (**Figure 24**). More than 90% of respondents mentioned that their clients prefer the issuance

Figure 23: Interest in Issuing Green Bonds

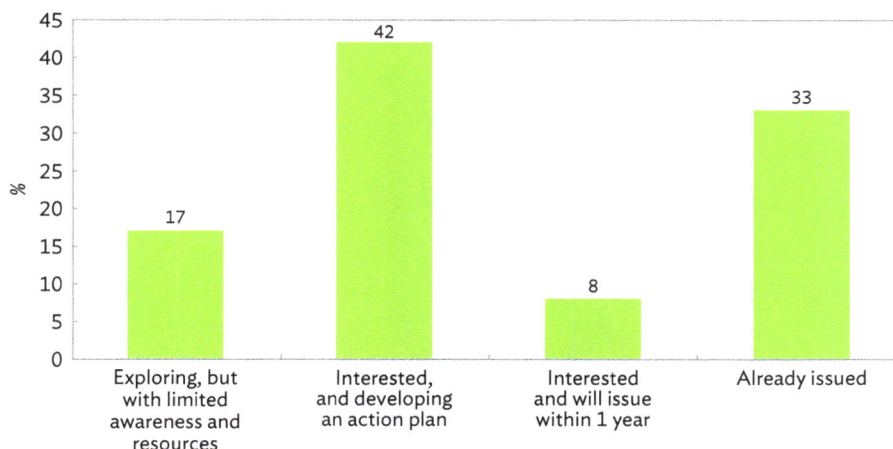

Source: Authors' compilation based on survey results.

Figure 24: Optimal Issuance Size

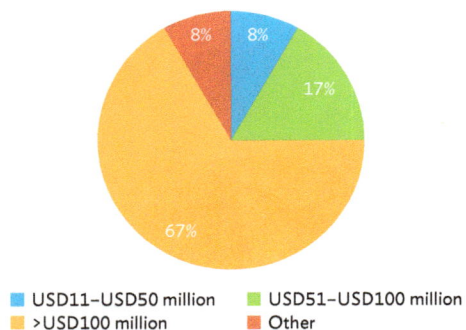

- ■ USD11–USD50 million
- ■ USD51–USD100 million
- ■ >USD100 million
- ■ Other

Source: Authors' compilation based on survey results.

green bonds over the next 3 years (**Figure 25**). Additionally, around 25% of respondents agreed that clean transportation and energy efficiency hold significant potential for the Thai green bond market's development. This finding is consistent with institutional investors' perspectives and the current composition of their green asset portfolios.

When asked why clients should issue green bonds, all respondents believe that it could result in lower funding costs. Around 75% of respondents believed this was the most compelling reason for companies to issue green bonds, while 25% believed it was a valid reason (**Figure 26**). Additionally, all respondents believed that issuing green bonds would improve the organization's green image and would be a key driver for issuers to incorporate ESG as part of corporate DNA. Furthermore, 75% of respondents agreed that green bonds could assist issuers in attracting new investors.

A respondent made an interesting but critical observation. Institutional investors such as commercial banks and insurance companies account for the lion's share of

of green bonds in Thai baht. It is important to note that the largest single issuance size among the 37 green bonds registered with the ThaiBMA was THB5.0 billion (approximately USD150 million), issued by BTS Group Holdings Public Company Limited on 24 May 2019. As of February 2022, green bonds issued in Thailand and registered with the ThaiBMA had an average issuance size of USD65 million.

In terms of sectors, all respondents agreed that renewable energy would present the greatest opportunity for Thailand to issue

Figure 25: Sectors That Are Most Promising Sectors for Green Bonds Issuance

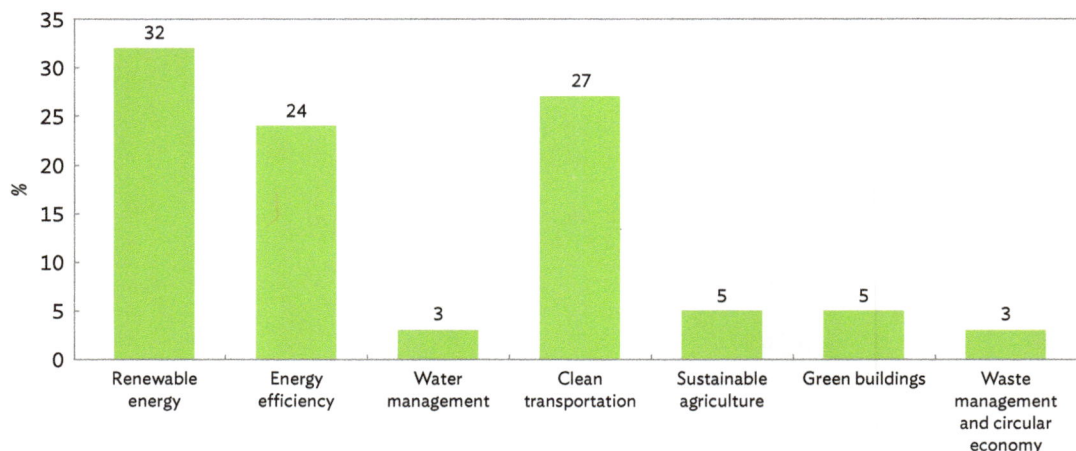

Source: Authors' compilation based on survey results.

Figure 26: Key Motivations for Issuing Green Bonds

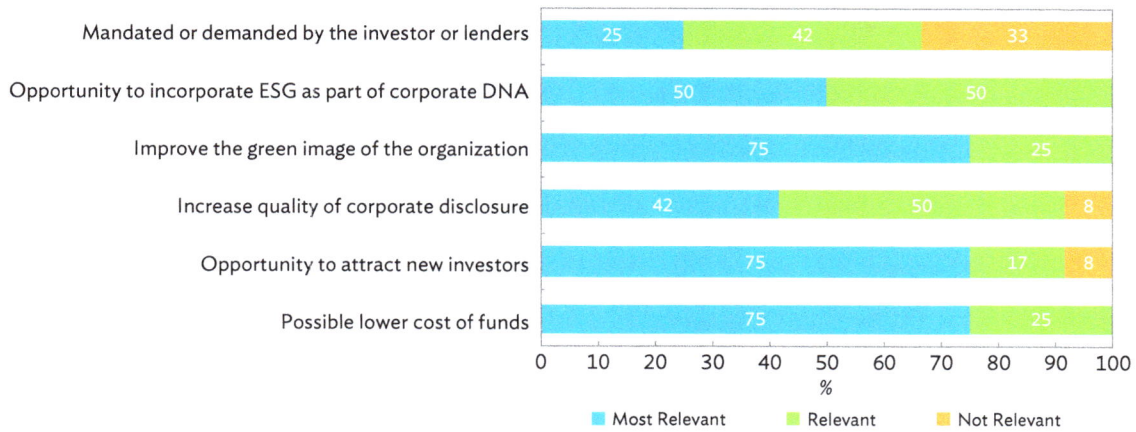

Motivation	Most Relevant	Relevant	Not Relevant
Mandated or demanded by the investor or lenders	25	42	33
Opportunity to incorporate ESG as part of corporate DNA	50	50	
Improve the green image of the organization	75	25	
Increase quality of corporate disclosure	42	50	8
Opportunity to attract new investors	75	17	8
Possible lower cost of funds	75	25	

ESG = environmental, social, and governance.
Source: Authors' compilation based on survey results.

investors in sustainable bonds. However, additional incentives, such as withholding tax reductions, should be considered to encourage retail investors to invest in sustainable bonds via mutual funds. Having a larger investor group focused on ESG investments could eventually result in a coupon rate reduction, which could offset issuers' additional costs.

Concerning market development, the majority of respondents identified a lack of eligible project pipelines as a clear impediment to their clients issuing green bonds (**Figure 27**). Another significant impediment was the absence of clear benefits of green bonds over conventional bonds, such as lower funding costs. One intriguing fact is that none of the

Figure 27: Main Obstacles Preventing Issuers from Investing Green Bonds

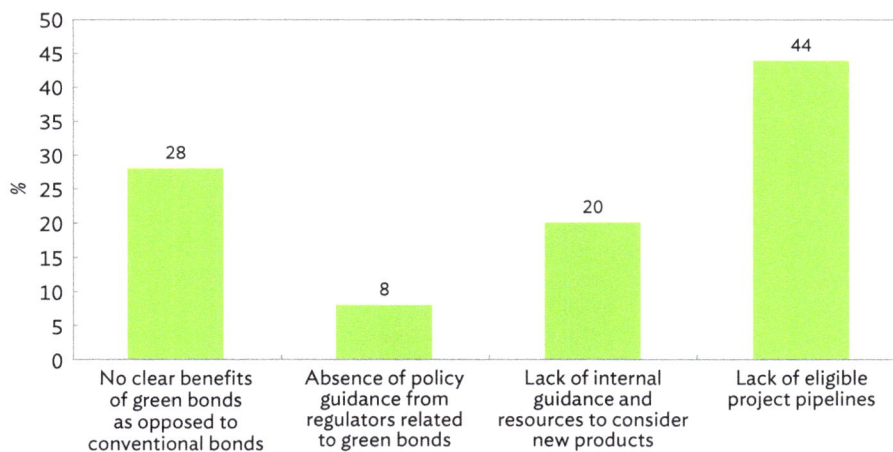

Obstacle	%
No clear benefits of green bonds as opposed to conventional bonds	28
Absence of policy guidance from regulators related to green bonds	8
Lack of internal guidance and resources to consider new products	20
Lack of eligible project pipelines	44

Source: Authors' compilation based on survey results.

respondents stated that they were unfamiliar with green bonds. Thus, the majority of market participants in Thailand appear to be familiar with the concept of green bonds, which is the critical issue preventing other issuers to come to the market: the identification of eligible green projects, assets, and/or expenditures that comply with the green labeling requirements.

Respondents were then asked to identify the primary policy mechanisms that would increase green bond issuance in Thailand. The majority of respondents indicated that increased investor demand would be the primary factor to consider, followed by incentives and/or subsidies for green bond issuers (**Figure 28**). While standardizing green taxonomies may provide clarity for green projects, slightly more than 30% of respondents identified this as a critical issue.

When asked about potential investors, nearly 80% of respondents believed that development partners such as ADB could significantly contribute to the development of the local green bond market by investing in green bonds issued by their clients (**Box 1**). Meanwhile, all

respondents agreed that insurance companies and financial institutions could invest in green bonds, with nearly 70% believing that insurance companies could play a significant role in facilitating the issuance of longer-term debt. Additionally, respondents believed that if retail investors gained a better understanding of ESG investing, they would be able to invest in green bonds via mutual funds, and that mutual funds could become significant investors (**Figure 29**).

Similar to institutional investors, underwriters and advisors believe that tax incentives for issuers and investors, as well as preferential purchasing from central banks, pension funds, and insurance companies, are necessary to further develop Thailand's green bond market (**Figure 30**). Respondents may have believed that local institutional investors—particularly central bank pension funds, social security funds, and insurance companies—have not yet communicated their commitments clearly. Respondents suggested that subsidy for bond labeling could persuade their clients to issue more green bonds, particularly for smaller issuers.

Figure 28: Key Drivers for Green Bonds Issuance

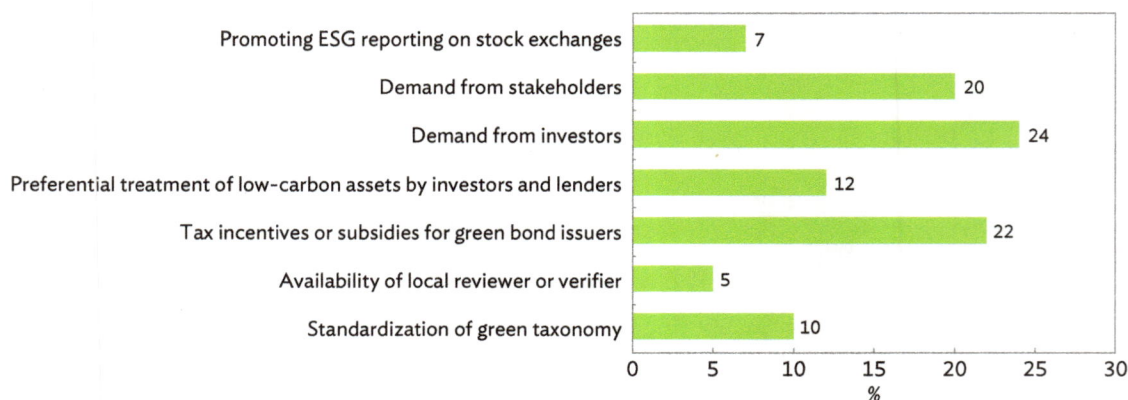

ESG = environmental, social, and governance.
Source: Authors' compilation based on survey results.

Box 1: The Asian Development Bank's Journey into Green Bonds and Blue Loans in Thailand

Sending a signal to the market that the bonds and loans supported by the Asian Development Bank (ADB) can be trusted is considered as one of the key value additions on labeled debt instruments. With our projects, we have ensured from the start that the labeled instruments we have invested in have a high level of integrity by supporting an independent review by a reputable verifier and encouraging certification by the Climate Bond Initiative, the gold standard for climate-aligned bonds and loans.

Our journey in Thailand started with the first certified climate bond issued in 2017 by B.Grimm Power Public Company Limited (B.Grimm). B.Grimm started its transition and diversification to renewable energy since 2015. ADB worked with the company to structure one-third of its overall USD465 million corporate bond issuance in 2017 as green bonds. We also played a key role in advising B.Grimm in ensuring compliance with internationally recognized Green Bond Standards and Climate Bond Standards, and facilitated the certification process—in addition to our investment in the bonds. In the process, ADB started to build in-house capability for advising clients in structuring green bonds with the aim of kickstarting a program to promote more green bond issuances, and to mobilize additional investors towards this emerging asset class.

Our next green bond involved a cornerstone investment in Energy Absolute's maiden green bond issuance used to support the financing of Thailand's biggest wind farm. The signing ceremony of the green bond was organized along with a large knowledge-sharing event at the Stock Exchange of Thailand, which was well attended by government decision-makers and planted the seeds for ADB's engagement with the Ministry of Finance and National Housing Authority to issue green, social, and sustainability bonds through the Association of Southeast Asian Nations Catalytic Green Finance Facility. After this, two Climate Bonds Initiative-certified green loans followed: (i) one to support ongoing renewable energy projects and the roll-out of an electric vehicle charging network in Thailand; and (ii) another to support a 257 megawatt solar project in Viet Nam, which was the first certified green loan in Viet Nam and the first certified green B-loan in Asia and the Pacific. Under ADB's B-loan program, ADB acts as lender of record, while commercial lenders provide funding and take full exposure on the borrower. A B-loan enables ADB to introduce new sources of financing to its clients, thereby mobilizing more funds for development projects.

From there, we started to expand the color spectrum with a USD100 million blue loan from ADB and Leading Asia's Private Infrastructure Fund to Indorama. This was ADB's first nonsovereign blue loan, following the Blue Natural Capital Financing Facility's Blue Bond Guidelines. The proceeds were used to reduce the environmental impact of plastic and to promote a circular economy by boosting the capacity of Indorama's plastic recycling plants in Thailand, the Philippines, Indonesia, and India.

Source: ADB.

Figure 29: Preferred Investors in Green Bonds

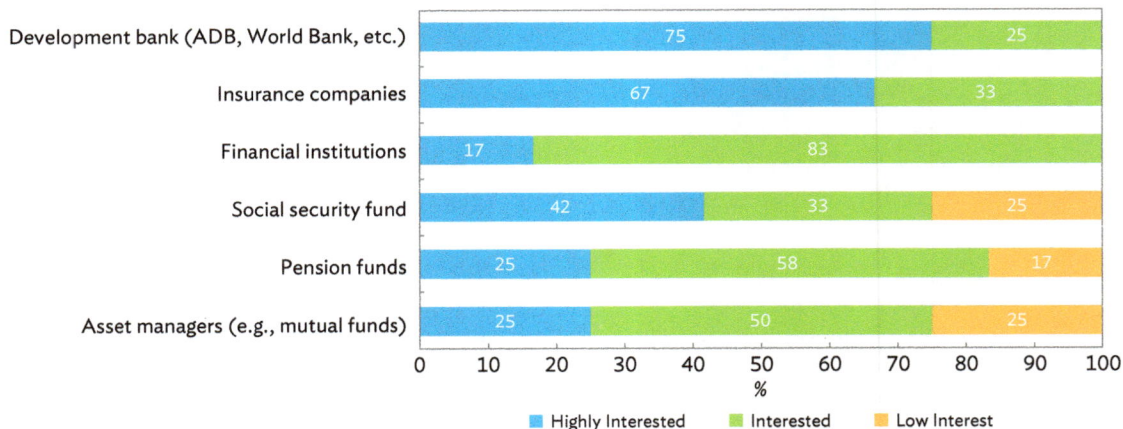

ADB = Asian Development Bank.
Source: Authors' compilation based on survey results.

Figure 30: Preferred Policy Options for Green Bond Market Development among Advisors and Underwriters

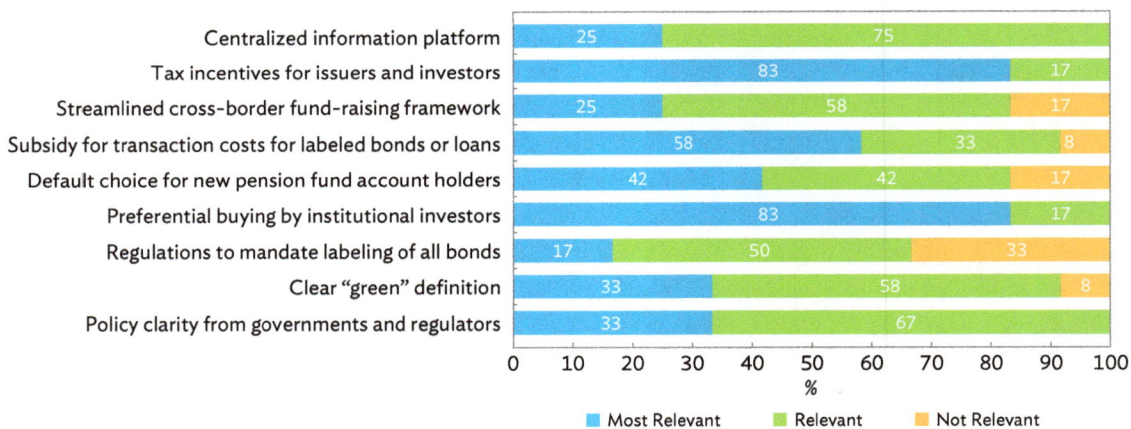

Source: Authors' compilation based on survey results.

While the SEC and ThaiBMA have provided incentives for the approval and registration of green bonds (as well as other types of sustainable bonds), more than 80% of respondents felt that this was insufficient and could be expanded further.

Meanwhile, more than 30% of respondents believed that mandating green bond labeling and external review may not be necessary as it could increase issuance costs, particularly pure-play issuers focused exclusively on green projects. But almost 100% of institutional investors believe that this element is critical because it provides them with proper assurance that the bonds in which they are investing are truly green.

In terms of capacity building, all respondents believe that chief financial officers of large corporations and listed companies would benefit from training to better understand green bonds and why they should include them in their financing strategy (**Figure 31**). Meanwhile, all respondents also believed that institutional investors should be trained to increase demand for green bonds. Indeed, 75% of respondents believed that training for these two groups of stakeholders is critical, while 25% believe it is necessary. All respondents agreed that deal teams within investment banks and, to a lesser extent, underwriters require training as well.

The majority of respondents believe that SLBs could be a critical driver in assisting brown businesses in becoming green (**Figure 32**). SLBs can enable companies operating in brown

industries to raise capital, establish relevant and ambitious key performance indicators and sustainability performance targets, and transition to a greener business model. This would enable these companies to participate in the sustainable finance journey and demonstrate their commitment to investors.

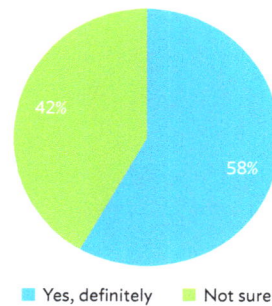

Figure 32: Potential of Sustainability-Linked Bonds to Turn Brown Companies Green

- Yes, definitely
- Not sure

Source: Authors' compilation based on survey results.

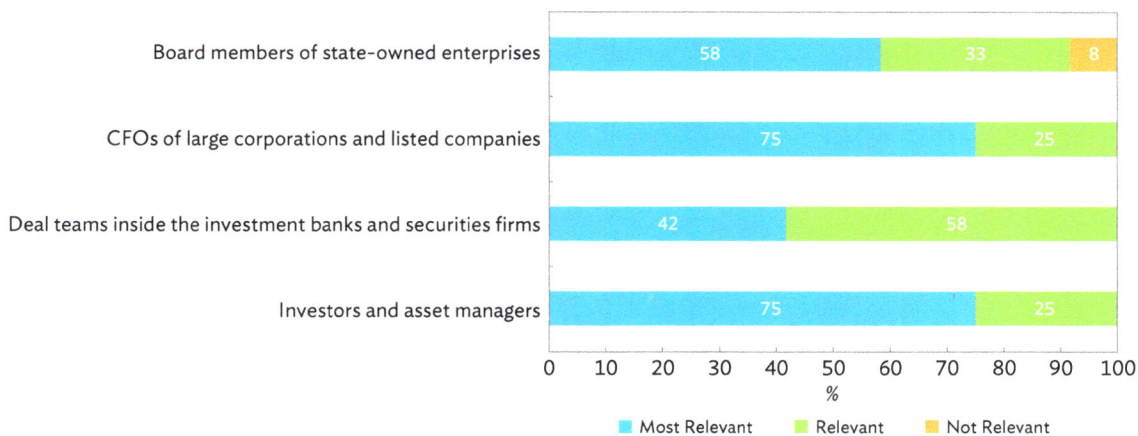

Figure 31: Capacity Building—Who Should be Trained?

	Most Relevant	Relevant	Not Relevant
Board members of state-owned enterprises	58	33	8
CFOs of large corporations and listed companies	75	25	
Deal teams inside the investment banks and securities firms	42	58	
Investors and asset managers	75	25	

CFO = chief financial officer.
Source: Authors' compilation based on survey results.

WHAT ADB CAN DO TO HELP

In the survey, respondents also identified several ways in which ADB could assist the Thai green bond market's development. These beneficial recommendations can be classified as follows.

As a Knowledge Partner

ADB could provide knowledge support to relevant stakeholders in Thailand, including potential issuers, capital market intermediaries, institutional investors, and the general public.

It is critical for potential issuers to understand that their operations can result in positive environmental and social developments. It is essential for institutional investors and the general public to understand that investing in green bonds is about more than yield. Incorporating nonfinancial ESG risks can have a material impact on their risk-adjusted returns and thus the long-term value of their assets under management. ADB can work with local regulators and industry associations to implement market awareness programs and host capacity-building workshops.

Additionally, ADB can provide technical assistance to relevant stakeholders in Thailand (**Box 2**). For example, providing guidance to potential issuers, arrangers, and underwriters throughout the issuance process is critical, as many issuers and their advisors are unfamiliar with the green bond issuance process, particularly with regard to identifying eligible projects, assets, and expenditures, as well as preparing the green bond framework.

ADB could also assist in providing market updates on the development of the sustainable bond market via *AsianBondsOnline*. To streamline issuances, a standardized framework for green bond issuance could be developed, such as a template for a green bond framework.

As an Investor

ADB can also act as an anchor investor to catalyze green bond market development. ADB could further invest in green bonds issued by local entities to broaden the investor base, while at the same time giving value on a "greenium."[16] Indeed, one respondent stated straightforwardly that ADB being an anchor investor in green bonds would be a critical factor because it would support investors' due diligence process and could imply whether an issuer meets the international standard.

Aside from acting as an investor, ADB could provide green loans to local businesses through syndication with local commercial banks. This could raise awareness among local commercial banks about the importance of ESG in their

---

[16] For many issuers, there is a benefit in terms of pricing for their green bond compared to other bonds that are not labeled. This price differential, which is often called a "greenium," is usually driven by the large demand for green bonds compared to the emerging supply.

operations and allow them to gain experience financing local businesses through green loans.

ADB can also provide credit guarantees for green bonds issued by local corporates. This would allow them to issue bonds with longer maturities to fund long-term projects. Furthermore, ADB may want to consider issuing green bonds locally in Thailand to finance ESG projects in both the public and private sectors.

Box 2: The Asian Development Bank's Technical Assistance to Support Thai Issuers and Underwriters

The Asian Development Bank (ADB) is implementing a regional technical assistance (TA) program to develop an ecosystem for sustainable local currency bond market development in ASEAN+3. Under the guidance of ASEAN+3 finance ministers and central bank governors, this TA was developed and implemented in accordance with the ASEAN+3 Asian Bond Markets Initiative's (ABMI) Medium-Term Road Map for 2019–2022. The TA program's overall activities are overseen by the Thai Ministry of Finance's Fiscal Policy Office and the People's Republic of China's Ministry of Finance as co-chairs of task force 1 of the ABMI. As a result, this TA program is truly owned by the ASEAN+3 governments.

Despite significant growth in the sustainable finance market as a result of innovative financial products and clear regulatory guidance, Thailand's sustainable bond market remains extremely small compared to the country's total local currency bond market. It was also highlighted in this survey that one of the key impediments to the development of Thailand's green bond market is a lack of project pipelines and issuers.

With the support of local regulatory bodies, this project aims to establish the necessary ecosystem for sustainable finance market development in Thailand. One of the key activities is to provide hands-on support to prospective issuers and underwriters to facilitate the issuance of sustainable bonds in Thailand, from the identification of eligible projects, assets, and expenditures to the preparation of green, social, and sustainability bond frameworks and discussions with external reviewers. Most recently, the TA assisted Thaifoods Group in launching the region's first social bond issued by a nonfinancial corporate in accordance with ASEAN Social Bond Standards.

ADB has been collaborating closely with TRIS Rating on this project, providing technical assistance in order for TRIS Rating to become Thailand's first Climate Bonds Initiative-accredited green bond verifier. We believe that the presence of a local external reviewer who is familiar with the local context, regulatory environment, and market practices is critical to the development of a sustainable finance market ecosystem. This would enable Thailand's sustainable finance market to further develop.

ADB would be happy to offer free consultation and provide technical hands-on support to Thai companies wishing to issue green, social, or sustainable bonds in Thailand. For interested entities, please contact Kosintr Puongsophol, financial sector specialist, ADB at kpuongsophol@adb.org.

Source: ADB.

FINAL WORD FROM SURVEY RESPONDENTS

The survey respondents were asked to give some final words on green bond market development in Thailand. The following are a few highlights:

- We have joint responsibility for our future by green financing.
- Knowledge sharing is very good (please keep doing it).
- Small to medium-size companies are also good potential issuers and need advice from experts.
- Awareness is a stepping-stone for change.
- "The best possible shot to save the one planet we've got" – Barack Obama.
- There are not many incentives compared with typical bonds.
- We need an agency to standardize the ESG rating.
- Emphasizing the importance of ESG by rewarding those who commit to do so will help accelerate the process. Some easy steps may work well, including awards recognition in the ESG area.
- The market is still very much driven by economic value rather than ESG aspects.
- We will definitely invest in green bonds.
- ESG-related investment would be an important factor in successfully achieving the SDGs.
- We are all responsible for sustainable development. Additional support from regulators, senior management, and the government is critical to advancing Thailand's strategy toward a net-zero transition.

- Regulators should establish key performance indicators to promote market activities, particularly demand-side activities. For example, mutual funds should have green or sustainable key performance indicators as part of their portfolio management.
- The investor community is generally well versed in ESG-related frameworks and will look to invest in green instruments when given a chance. Establishing a green taxonomy for the country will be a crucial enabler.
- More issuers will need to be enabled to issue green instruments, through capability building, but also initial support would be defraying expenses in establishing a green framework as well as external review costs to reduce barriers to entry. Once such frameworks are in place, and green issuances become routine and familiar, companies will see the value of tapping into the green market on an ongoing basis. Such support could be provided in terms of special grants and/or tax deduction incentives.
- We agree that ADB could play a crucial role in assisting Thailand's green bond market's development. In addition to its role as a knowledge partner, technical assistance provider, and investor, we see an important role for ADB as a guarantor to improve issuers' credit rating. This is in line with investors' identified investment priorities, which place importance on credit ratings.

NEXT STEPS

This survey revealed that the majority of respondents are committed to becoming more environmentally friendly, both from an investor and an underwriter perspective. Additional efforts, however, are required, particularly in terms of capacity building for relevant stakeholders, the expansion of the eligible project pipeline and issuer base, and greater incentives (including technical assistance) from development partners. Currently, Thailand's green bond market is dominated by three sectors: renewable energy, energy efficiency, and clean transportation. It is critical to further diversify and explore issuers from other promising sectors—such as green buildings, sustainable agriculture, and waste management—to provide them with more funding opportunities and to give investors more investment opportunities.

As secretariat of the ABMI, ADB will continue to work closely with local regulatory bodies to establish and strengthen the ecosystem necessary for Thailand's sustainable finance market's development, including capacity building, the publication of guidance and handbooks, and technical assistance to issuers on their sustainable finance journey.

www.ingramcontent.com/pod-product-compliance
Lightning Source LLC
Chambersburg PA
CBHW050057220326
41599CB00045B/7448